The night was mild again, as in the year before. The snow lay like white powder on the hard earth; the moon was full, and the street was a length of dazzling silence. The lighted candle was in the parlor window, shining toward the meeting-house, the fire burned brightly on the hearth, the front door was ajar. Letty wrapped her old cape round her shoulders, drew her hood over her head, and seated herself at the window....

And then a footstep, drawing ever nearer, sounded crunch, crunch in the snow. Letty pushed her chair back into the shadow. The footstep halted at the gate, came falteringly up the path, turned aside and came nearer the window. Then a voice said: "Don't be frightened, Letty...."

++

Also by Kate Douglas Wiggin:

THE STORY OF PATSY
THE BIRDS' CHRISTMAS CAROL*
A SUMMER IN A CANON
TIMOTHY'S QUEST
POLLY OLIVER'S PROBLEM
A CATHEDRAL COURTSHIP AND PENELOPE'S ENGLISH
    EXPERIENCES
THE VILLAGE WATCH-TOWER
MARM LISA
PENELOPE'S PROGRESS
PENELOPE'S IRISH EXPERIENCES
DIARY OF A GOOSE GIRL
REBECCA OF SUNNYBROOK FARM
ROSE O' THE RIVER
NEW CHRONICLES OF REBECCA
THE OLD PEABODY PEW
SUSANNA AND SUE
MOTHER CAREY'S CHICKENS
THE STORY OF WAITSTILL BAXTER
PENELOPE'S POSTSCRIPTS
LADIES IN WAITING
MY GARDEN OF MEMORY
CREEPING JENNY, and OTHER NEW ENGLAND STORIES

*Published by Ballantine/Epiphany Books

THE ROMANCE

of a

CHRISTMAS CARD

Kate Douglas Wiggin

BALLANTINE BOOKS • NEW YORK

Published in the United States of America by Ballantine Books, a division of Random House, Inc., New York, and simultaneously in Canada by Random House of Canada Limited, Toronto.

ISBN 0-345-36003-6

Manufactured in the United States of America

First Ballantine Books Edition: December 1989

I

IT was Christmas Eve and a Saturday night when Mrs. Larrabee, the Beulah minister's wife, opened the door of the study where her husband was deep in the revision of his next day's sermon, and thrust in her comely head framed in a knitted rigolette.

"Luther, I'm going to run down to Letty's. We think the twins are going to have measles; it's the only thing they have n't had, and Letty's spirits are not up to concert pitch. You look like a blessed old prophet tonight, my dear! What's the text?"

The minister pushed back his spectacles and ruffled his gray hair.

"Isaiah 6:8: *And I heard the voice of the Lord saying, 'Whom shall I send?' . . . Then I said, 'Here am I! Send me!'.*"

+++

"It does n't sound a bit like Christmas, some-how."

"It has the spirit, if it has n't the sound," said the minister. "There is always so little spare money in the village that we get less and less accustomed to sharing what we have with others. I want to remind the people that there are differ-ent ways of giving, and that the bestowing of one's self in service and good deeds can be the best of all gifts. Letty Boynton won't need the sermon!—Don't be late, Reba."

"Of course not. When was I ever late? It has just struck seven and I'll be back by eight to choose the hymns. And oh! Luther, I have some fresh ideas for Christmas cards and I am going to try my luck with them in the marts of trade. There are hundreds of thousands of such things sold nowadays; and if the 'Boston Banner' likes my verses well enough to send me the paper reg-ularly, why should n't the people who make cards like them too, especially when I can draw and paint my own pictures?"

"I've no doubt they'll like them; who would n't? If the parish knew what a ready pen you have, they'd suspect that you help me in my sermons! The question is, will the publishers send you a check, or only a copy of your card?"

"I should relish a check, I confess; but oh! I should like almost as well a beautifully colored card, Luther, with a picture of my own inventing on it, my own verse, and R.L. in tiny letters somewhere in the corner! It would make such a lovely Christmas present! And I should be so proud; inside of course, not outside! I would cover my halo with my hat so that nobody in the congregation would ever notice it!"

The minister laughed.

"Consult Letty, my dear. David used to be in some sort of picture business in Boston. She will know, perhaps, where to offer your card!"

At the introduction of a new theme into the conversation Mrs. Larrabee slipped into a chair by the door, her lantern swinging in her hand.

"David can't be as near as Boston or we should hear of him sometimes. A pretty sort of brother to be meandering foot-loose over the earth, and Letty working her fingers to the bone to support his children—twins at that! It was just like David Gilman to have twins! Does n't it seem incredible that he can let Christmas go by without a message? I dare say he does n't even remember that his babies were born on Christmas

Eve. To be sure he is only Letty's half-brother, but after all they grew up together and are nearly the same age."

"You always judged David a little severely, Reba. Don't despair of reforming any man till you see the grass growing over his bare bones. I always have a soft spot in my heart for him when I remember his friendship for Dick; but that was before your time.—Oh! these boys, these boys!" The minister's voice quavered. "We give them our very life-blood. We love them, cherish them, pray over them, do our best to guide them, yet they take the path that leads from home. In some way, God knows how, we fail to call out the return love, or even the filial duty and respect!—Well, we won't talk about it, Reba; my business is to breathe the breath of life into my text: 'Here am I, Lord, send me!' Letty certainly continues to say it heroically, whatever her troubles."

"Yes, Letty is so ready for service that she will always be sent, till the end of time; but if David ever has an interview with his Creator I can hear him say: 'Here am I, Lord; send Letty!'"

The minister laughed again. He laughed freely and easily nowadays. His first wife had been a sort of understudy for a saint, and after a

brief but depressing connubial experience she
had died, leaving him with a boy of six; a boy
who already, at that tender age, seemed to cherish a passionate aversion to virtue in any form—
the result, perhaps, of daily doses of the
catechism administered by an abnormally pious
mother.

The minister had struggled valiantly with his
paternal and parochial cares for twelve lonely
years when he met, wooed, and won (very much
to his astonishment and exaltation) Reba Crosby.
There never was a better bargain driven! She was
forty-five by the family Bible but twenty-five in
face, heart, and mind, while he would have been
printed as sixty in "Who's Who in New Hampshire" although he was far older in patience and
experience and wisdom. The minister was spiritual, frail, and a trifle prone to self-deprecation;
the minister's new wife was spirited, vigorous,
courageous, and clever. She was also Western-
born, college-bred, good as gold, and invincibly,
incurably cheerful. The minister grew younger
every year, for Reba doubled his joys and halved
his burdens, tossing them from one of her fine
shoulders to the other as if they were feathers.
She swept into the quiet village life of Beulah
like a salt sea breeze. She infused a new spirit

into the bleak church "sociables" and made them positively agreeable functions. The choir ceased from wrangling, the Sunday School plucked up courage and flourished like a green bay tree. She managed the deacons, she braced up the missionary societies, she captivated the parish, she cheered the depressed and depressing old ladies and cracked jokes with the invalids.

"Ain't she a little mite too jolly for a minister's wife?" questioned Mrs. Ossian Popham, who was a professional pessimist.

"If this world is a place of want, woe, wantonness, an' wickedness, same as you claim, Maria, I don't see how a minister's wife *can* be too jolly!" was her husband's cheerful reply. "Look how she's melted up the ice in both congregations, so't the other church is most willin' we should prosper, so long as Mis' Larrabee stays here an' we don't get too fur ahead of 'em in attendance. Me for the smiles, Maria!"

And Osh Popham was right; for Reba Larrabee convinced the members of the rival church (the rivalry between the two being in rigidity of creed, not in persistency in good works) that there was room in heaven for at least two denominations; and said that if they could n't unite in this world, perhaps they'd get round to it in the next. Finally, she saved Letitia Boynton's soul alive by giving her a warm, understanding friendship, and she even contracted to win back the minister's absent son some time or other, and convince him of the error of his ways.

"Let Dick alone a little longer, Luther," she would say; "don't hurry him, for he won't come home so long as he's a failure; it would please the village too much, and Dick hates the village. He does n't accept our point of view, that we must love our enemies and bless them that despitefully use us. The village did despitefully use Dick, and for that matter, David Gilman too. They were criticized, gossiped about, judged without mercy. Nobody believed in them, nobody ever praised them;—and what is that about praise being the fructifying sun in which our virtues ripen, or something like that? I'm not quoting it right, but I wish I'd said it. They were called wild when most of their wildness was exuberant vitality; their mistakes were magnified, their mad pranks exaggerated. If I'd been married to you, my dear, while Dick was growing up, I would n't have let you keep him here in this little backwater of life; he needed more room, more movement. They would n't have been so down on him in Racine, Wisconsin!"

Mrs. Larrabee lighted her lantern, closed the door behind her, and walked briskly down the lonely road that led from the parsonage at Beulah Corner to Letitia Boynton's house. It was bright moonlight and the ground was covered with lightfallen snow, but the lantern habit was a fixed one among Beulah ladies, who, even when they were not widows or spinsters, made their evening calls mostly without escort. The light of a lantern not only enabled one to pick the better side of a bad road, but would illuminate the face of any male stranger who might be of a burglarious or murderous disposition. Reba Larrabee was not a timid person; indeed, she was wont to say that men were so scarce in Beulah that unless they were out-and-out ruffians it would be an inspiration to meet a few, even if it were only to pass them in the middle of the road.

There was a light in the meeting-house as she passed, and then there was a long stretch of shining white silence unmarked by any human habitation till she came to the tumble-down black cottage inhabited by "Door Button" Davis, as the little old man was called in the village. In the distance she could see Osh Popham's two-story house brilliantly illuminated by kerosene lamps, and as she drew nearer she even descried Ossian himself, seated at the cabinet organ in his shirt-sleeves, practicing the Christmas anthem, his daughter holding a candle to the page while she struggled to adjust a circuitous alto to her father's tenor. On the hither side of the Popham house, and quite obscured by it, stood Letitia Boynton's one-story gray cottage. It had a clump of tall cedar trees for background and the bare branches of the elms in front were hung lightly with snow garlands. As Mrs. Larrabee came closer, she set down her lantern and looked fixedly at the familiar house as if something new arrested her gaze.

"It looks like a little night-light!" she thought. "And how queer of Letty to be sitting at the open window!"

Nearer still she crept, yet not so near as to startle her friend. A tall brass candlestick, with a lighted tallow candle in it, stood on the table in the parlor window; but the room in which Letty sat was unlighted save by the fire on the hearth, which gleamed brightly behind the quaint and-irons—Hessian soldiers of iron, painted in bright colors. Over the mantel hung the portrait of Letty's mother, a benign figure clad in black silk, the handsome head topped by a snowy muslin cap with floating strings. Just round the corner of the fireplace was a half-open door leading into a tiny bedroom, and the flickering flame lighted the heads of two sleeping children, arms interlocked, bright tangled curls flowing over one pillow.

Letty herself sat in a low chair by the open window wrapped in an old cape of ruddy brown homespun, from the folds of which her delicate head rose like a flower in a bouquet of autumn leaves. One elbow rested on the table; her chin in the cup of her hand. Her head was turned away a little so that one could see only the knot of bronze hair, the curve of a cheek, and the sweep of an eyelash.

"What a picture!" thought Reba. "The very thing for my Christmas card! It would do almost without a change, if only she is willing to let me use her."

"Wake up, Letty!" she called. "Come and let me in!—Why, your front door is n't closed!"

"The fire smoked a little when I first lighted it," said Letty, rising when her friend entered, and then softly shutting the bedroom door that the children might not waken. "The night is so mild and the room so warm, I could n't help opening the window to look at the moon on the snow. Sit down, Reba! How good of you to come when you've been rehearsing for the Christmas Tree exercises all the afternoon."

II

"IT'S never 'good' of me to come to talk with you, Letty!" And the minister's wife sank into a comfortable seat and took off her rigolette. "Enough virtue has gone out of me to-day to Christianize an entire heathen nation! Oh! how I wish Luther would go and preach to a tribe of cannibals somewhere, and make me superintendent of the Sunday-School! How I should like to deal, just for a change, with some simple problem like the undesirability and indigestibility involved in devouring your next-door neighbor! Now I pass my life in saying, 'Love your neighbor as yourself'; which is far more difficult than to say, 'Don't *eat* your neighbor, it's such a disgusting habit,—and wrong besides,'—though I dare say they do it half the time because the market

++++++++++++++++++++++++++++++++++++++

is bad. The first thing I'd do would be to get my cannibals to raise sheep. If they ate more mutton, they would n't eat so many missionaries."

Letty laughed. "You're so funny, Reba dear, and I was so sad before you came in. Don't let the minister take you to the cannibals until after I die!"

"No danger!—Letty, do you remember I told you I'd been trying my hand on some verses for a Christmas card?"

"Yes; have you sent them anywhere?"

"Not yet. I could n't think of the right decoration and color scheme and was afraid to trust it all to the publishers. Now I've found just what I need for one of them, and you gave it to me, Letty!"

"I?"

"Yes, you; to-night, as I came down the road. The house looked so quaint, backed by the dark cedars, and the moon and the snow made everything dazzling. I could see the firelight through the open window, the Hessian soldier andirons, you mother's portrait, the children asleep in the next room, and you, wrapped in your cape waiting or watching for something or somebody."

"I was n't watching or waiting! I was dream-
ing," said Letty hurriedly.

"You looked as if you were watching, anyway,
and I thought if I were painting the picture I
would call it 'Expectancy,' or 'The Vigil,' or
'Sentry Duty.' However, when I make you into a
card, Letty, nobody will know what the figure at
the window means, till they read my verses."

"I'll give you the house, the room, the andirons, and even mother's portrait, but you don't
mean that you want to put *me* on the card?" And
Letty turned like a startled deer as she rose and
brushed a spark from the hearth-rug.

"No, not the whole of you, of course, though
I'm not clever enough to get a likeness even if I
wished. I merely want to make a color sketch of
your red-brown cape, your hair that matches it,
your ear, an inch of cheek, and the eyelashes of
one eye, if you please, ma'am."

"That does n't sound quite so terrifying." And
Letty looked more manageable.

"Nobody'll ever know that a real person sat at
a real window and that I saw her there; but when
I send the card with a finished picture, and my
verses beautifully lettered on it, the printing
people will be more likely to accept it."

"And if they do, shall I have a dozen to give to my Bible-class?" asked Letty in a wheedling voice.

"You shall have more than that! I'm willing to divide my magnificent profits with you. You will have furnished the picture and I the verses. It's wonderful, Letty,—it's providential! You just *are* a Christmas card to-night! It seems so strange that you even put the lighted candle in the window when you never heard my verse. The candle caught my eye first, and I remembered the Christmas customs we studied for the church festival,—the light to guide the Christ Child as he walks through the dark streets on the Eve of Mary."

"Yes, I thought of that," said Letty, flushing a little. "I put the candle there first so that the house should n't be all dark when the Pophams went by to choir-meeting, and just then I—I remembered, and was glad I did it!"

"These are my verses, Letty." And Reba's voice was soft as she turned her face away and looked at the flames mounting upward in the chimney:—

My door is on the latch to-night,
The hearth fire is aglow.

I seem to hear swift passing feet,—
    The Christ Child in the snow.

My heart is open wide to-night
    For stranger, kith or kin.
I would not bar a single door
    Where Love might enter in!

There was a moment's silence and Letty broke it. "It means the sort of love the Christ Child brings, with peace and goodwill in it. I'm glad to be a part of that card, Reba, so long as nobody knows me, and—"

Here she made an impetuous movement and, covering her eyes with her hands, burst into a despairing flood of confidence, the words crowding each other and tumbling out of her mouth as if they feared to be stopped.

"After I put the candle on the table . . . I could not rest for thinking . . . I was n't ready in my soul to light the Christ Child on his way . . . I was bitter and unresigned . . . It is three years to-night since the children were born . . . and each year I have hoped and waited and waited and hoped, thinking that David might remember. David! My brother, their father! Then the fire on the hearth, the moon and the snow quieted me, and I felt that I wanted to open the door, just a little. No one will notice that it's ajar, I thought, but there's a touch of welcome in it, anyway. And after a few minutes I said to myself: 'It's no use, David won't come; but I'm glad the firelight shines on mother's picture, for he loved mother, and if she had n't died when he was scarcely more then a boy, things might have been different. . . . The reason I opened the bed-room door—something I never do when the babies are asleep—was because I needed a sight of their faces to reconcile me to my duty and take the resentment out of my heart . . . and it did flow out, Reba,—out into the stillness. It is so dazzling white outside, I could n't bear my heart to be shrouded in gloom!"

"Poor Letty!" And Mrs. Larrabee furtively wiped away a tear. "How long since you have heard? I did n't dare ask."

"Not a word, not a line for nearly three months, and for the half-year before that it was nothing but a note, sometimes with a five-dollar bill enclosed. David seems to think it the natural thing for me to look after his children; as if there could be no question of any life of my own."

"You began wrong, Letty. You were born a

prop and you've been propping somebody ever since."

"I've done nothing but my plain duty. When my mother died there was my stepfather to nurse, but I was young and strong; I did n't mind; and he was n't a burden long, poor father. Then, after four years came the shock of David's reckless marriage. When he asked if he might bring that girl here until her time of trial was over, it seemed to me I could never endure it! But there were only two of us left, David and I; I thought of mother and said yes."

"I remember, Letty; I had come to Beulah then."

"Yes, and you know what Eva was. How David, how anybody, could have loved her, I cannot think! Well, he brought her, and you know how it turned out. David never saw her alive again, nor ever saw his babies after they were three days old. Still, what can you expect of a father who is barely twenty-one?"

"If he's old enough to have children, he's old enough to notice them," said Mrs. Larrabee with her accustomed spirit. "Somebody ought to jog his sense of responsibility. It's wrong for women to assume men's burdens beyond a certain point;

it only makes them more selfish. If you only knew where David is, you ought to bundle the children up and express them to his address. Not a word of explanation or apology; simply tie a tag on them, saying, 'Here's your Twins!'"

"But I love the babies," said Letty smiling through her tears, "and David may not be in a position to keep them."

"Then he should n't have had them," retorted Reba promptly; "especially not two of them. There's such a thing as a man's being too lavish with babies when he has no intention of doing anything for them but bring them into the world. If you had a living income, it would be one thing, but it makes me burn to have you stitching on coats to feed and clothe your half-brother's children!"

"Perhaps it does n't make any difference— now!" sighed Letty, pushing back her hair with an abstracted gesture. "I gave up a good deal for the darlings once, but that's past and gone. Now, after all, they're the only life I have, and I'd rather make coats for them than for myself."

Letty Boynton had never said so much as this to Mrs. Larrabee in the three years of their friendship, and on her way back to the parsonage, the minister's wife puzzled a little over the

look in Letty's face when she said, "David
seemed to think there could be no question of
any life of my own"; and again, "I gave up a
good deal for the darlings once!"

"Luther," she said to the minister, when the
hymns had been chosen, the sermon pronounced
excellent, and they were toasting their toes over
the sitting-room fire,—"Luther, do you suppose
there ever was anything between Letty Boynton
and Dick?"

"No," he answered reflectively, "I don't think
so. Dick always admired Letty and went to the
house a great deal, but I imagine that was chiefly
for David's sake, for they were as like as peas in a
pod in the matter of mischief. If there had been
more than friendship between Dick and Letty,
Dick would never have gone away from Beulah,
or if he had gone, he surely would have come
back to see how Letty fared. A fellow yearns for
news of the girl he loves even when he is content
to let silence reign between him and his old father.—What makes you think there was anything particular, Reba?"

"What makes anybody think anything!—I
wonder why some people are born props, and
others leaners or twiners? I believe the very
nursing-bottle leaned heavily against Letty

when she lay on her infant pillow. I did n't know her when she was a child, but I believe that when she was eight all the other children of three and five in the village looked to her for support and guidance!"

"It's a great vocation—that of being a prop," smiled the minister, as he peeled a red Baldwin apple, carefully preserving the spiral and eating it first.

"I suppose the wobbly vine thinks it's grand to be a stout trellis when it needs one to climb on, but does n't the trellis ever want to twine, I wonder?" And Reba's tone was doubtful.

"Even the trellis leans against the house, Reba."

"Well, Letty never gets a chance either to lean or to twine! Her family, her friends, her acquaintances, even the stranger within her gates, will pass trees, barber poles, telephone and telegraph poles, convenient corners of buildings, fence posts, ladders, and lightning rods for the sake of winding their weakness around her strength. When she sits down from sheer exhaustion, they come and prop themselves against her back. If she goes to bed, they climb up on the footboard, hang a drooping head, and look her wistfully in

the eye for sympathy. Prop on, prop ever, seems
to be the underlying law of the universe!"

"Poor Reba! She is talking of Letty and thinking of herself!" And the minister's eye twinkled.

"Well, a little!" admitted his wife; "but I'm
only a village prop, not a family one. Where you
are concerned"—and she administered an affec-
tionate pat to his cheek as she rose from her
chair—"I'm a trellis that leans against a rock!"

III

ETITIA BOYNTON's life had been rather a drab one as seen through other people's eyes, but it had never seemed so to her till within the last few years. Her own father had been the village doctor, but of him she had no memory. Her mother's second marriage to a venerable country lawyer, John Gilman, had brought a kindly, inefficient stepfather into the family, a man who speedily became an invalid needing constant nursing. The birth of David when Letty was three years old, brought a new interest into the household, and the two children grew to be fast friends; but when Mrs. Gilman died, and Letty found herself at eighteen the mistress of the house, the nurse of her aged stepfather, and the only guardian of a boy of fifteen, life became difficult. More difficult still it became when the old lawyer died, for he at least had been a sort of fictitious head of the family and his mere existence kept David within bounds.

David was a lively, harum-scarum, handsome youth, good at his lessons, popular with his companions, always in a scrape, into which he was generally drawn by the minister's son, so the neighbors thought. At any rate, Dick Larrabee, as David's senior, received the lion's share of the blame when mischief was abroad. If Parson Larrabee's boy could n't behave any better than an unbelieving blacksmith's, a Methodist farmer's, or a Baptist storekeeper's, what was the use of claiming superior efficacy for the Congregational form of belief?

"Dick's father's never succeeded in bringing him into the church, though he's worked on him from the time he was knee-high to a toad," said Mrs. Popham.

"P'raps his mother kind o' vaccinated him with religion 'stid o' leavin' him to take it the natural way, as the ol' sayin' is," was her husband's response. "The first Mis' Larrabee was as good as gold, but she may have overdone the trick a little mite, mebbe; and what's more, I kind o' suspicion the parson thinks so himself.

He ain't never been quite the same since Dick left home, 'cept in preachin'; an' I tell you, Maria, his highwater mark there is higher 'n ever. Abel Dunn o' Boston walked home from meetin' with me Thanksgivin', an', says he, takin' off his hat an' moppin' his forehead, 'Osh,' says he, 'does your minister preach like that every Sunday?' 'No,' says I, 'he don't. If he did we could n't stan' it! He preaches like that about once a month, an' we don't care what he says the rest o' the time.'"

"Well, so far as boys are concerned, preachin' ain't so reliable, for behavin' purposes, as a good young alder switch," was the opinion of Mrs. Popham, her children being of the comatose kind, whose minds had never been illuminated by the dazzling idea of disobedience.

"Land sakes, Maria! There ain't alders enough on the river-bank to switch religion into a boy like Dick Larrabee. It's got to come like a thief in the night, as the ol' sayin' is, but I guess I don't mean thief, I guess I mean star: it's got to come kind o' like a star in a dark night. If the whole village, 'generate an' onregenerate, had n't 'a' kep' on naggin' an' hectorin' an' criticizin' them two boys, Dick an' Dave,—carryin' tales an' multiplyin' of 'em by two, *'ong root,'* as the ol' sayin' is,—I dare say they'd 'a' both been here yet; 'stid o' roamin' roun' the earth seekin' whom they may devour."

There was considerable truth in Ossian Popham's remark, as Letty could have testified; for the conduct of the Boynton-Gilman household, as well as that of the minister, had been continually under inspection and discussion.

Nothing could remain long hidden in Beulah. Nobody spied, nobody pried, nobody listened at doors or windows, nobody owned a microscope, nobody took any particular notice of events, or if they did they preserved an attitude of profound indifference while doing it,—yet everything was known sooner or later. The amount of the fish and meat bill, the precise extent of credit, the number of letters in the post, the amount of fuel burned, the number of absences from church and prayer-meeting, the calls or visits made and received, the hours of arrival or departure, the source of all incomes,—these details were the common property of the village. It even took cognizance of more subtle things, for it observed and recorded the fluctuations of all love affairs, and the fluctuations also in the religious experiences of various persons not always in spiritual equilibrium; for the soul was an object of scru-

tiny in Beulah, as well as mind, body, and es-
tate.

Letty Boynton used to feel that nothing was
exclusively her own; that she belonged to Beulah
part and parcel; but Dick Larrabee was far more
restive under the village espionage than were she
and David.

It was natural that David should want to leave
Beulah and make his way in the world, and his
sister did not oppose it. Dick's circumstances
were different. He had inherited a small house
and farm from his mother, had enjoyed a college
education, and had been offered a share in a good
business in a city twelve miles away. He left
Beulah because he hated it. He left because he
could not endure his father's gentle remon-
strances or the bewilderment in his stepmother's
eyes. She was a newcomer in the household and
her glance seemed to say: "Why on earth do you
behave so badly to your father when you're such
a delightful chap?" He left because Deacon Todd
had prayed for him publicly at a Christian En-
deavor meeting; because Mrs. Popham had cir-
culated a wholly baseless scandal about him; and
finally because in his young misery the only
being who could have comforted him by joining
her hapless fortunes to his had refused to do so.

He did n't know why. He had always counted on
Letty when the time should come to speak the
word. He had shown his heart in everything but
words; what more did a girl want? Of course, if
any one preferred a purely fantastic duty to a
man's love, and allowed a scapegrace brother to
foist two red-faced, squalling babies on her,
there was nothing to be said. So, in this frame of
mind he had had one flaming, passionate,
wrong-headed scene with his father, and strode
out of Beulah with dramatic gestures of shaking
its dust off his feet. His father, roused for once
from his lifelong patience, had been rather terrible in that last scene; so terrible that he had
never forgiven himself, or really believed himself
fully forgiven by God, though his son had alien-
ated half the village and nearly rent the parish in
twain by his conduct.

As for Letty, she held her peace. She could
only hope that the minister and his wife sus-
pected nothing, and she was sure of Beulah's
point of view. That a girl would never give up a
suitor, if she had any hope of tying him to her
for life, was a popular form of belief in the com-
munity; and strangely enough it was chiefly the
women, not the men, who made it current. Now
and then a soft-hearted and chivalrous male

would observe indulgently of some village
beauty, "I should n't wonder a mite if she could
'a' had Bill for the askin'"; but this opinion
would be met by such a chorus of feminine incredulity that its author generally withdrew it as
unsound and untenable.

It was then, when Dick had gone away, that
the days had grown drab and long, but the twins
kept Letty's inexperienced hands busy, though in
the first year she had the help of old Miss Clarissa Perry, a childless expert in the bringing-up
of babies.

The friendship of Reba Larrabee, so bright
and cheery and comprehending, was a never-
ending solace. There was nothing of the martyr
about Letty. She was not wholly resigned to her
lot, and to tell the truth she did not intend to
be, for a good many years yet.

"I'm not a minister, but I'm the wife of a
minister, which is the next best thing," Mrs.
Larrabee used to say. "I tell you, Letty, there's no
use in human creatures being resigned till their
bodies are fairly worn out with fighting. When
you can't think of another mortal thing to do, be
resigned; but I'm convinced that the Lord is
ashamed of us when we fold our hands too soon!"

"You were born courageous, Reba!" And Letty

would look admiringly at the rosy cheeks and bright eyes of her friend.

"My blood circulates freely; that helps me a lot. Everybody's blood circulates in Racine, Wisconsin."—And the minister's wife laughed genially. "Yours, hereabouts, freezes up in your six months of cold weather, and when it begins to thaw out the snow is ready to fall again. That sort of thing induces depression, although no mere climate would account for Mrs. Popham.—Ossian said to Luther the other day: 'Maria ain't hardly to blame, parson. She come from a gloomy stock. The Ladds was all gloomy, root and branch. They say that the Ladd babies was always discouraged two days after they was born.'"

The cause of Letty's chief heartache, the one that she could reveal to nobody, was that her brother should leave her nowadays so completely to her own resources. She recalled the time when he came home from Boston, pale, haggard, ashamed, and told her of his marriage, months before. She could read in his lack-lustre eyes, and hear in his voice, the absence of love, the fear of the future. That was bad enough, but presently he said: "Letty, there's more to tell. I've no money, and no place to put my wife, but

there's a child coming. Can I bring her here till
—afterwards? You won't like her, but she's so
ailing and despondent just now that I think
she'll behave herself, and I'll take her away as
soon as she's able to travel. She would never stay
here in the country, anyway; you could n't hire
her to do it."

She came: black-haired, sullen-faced Eva,
with a vulgar beauty of her own, much damaged
by bad temper, discontent, and illness. Oh,
those terrible weeks for Letty, hiding her own
misery, putting on a brave face with the neighbors, keeping the unwelcome sister-in-law in the
background.

It was bitterly cold, and Eva raged against the
climate, the house, the lack of a servant, the
absence of gayety, and above all at the prospect
of motherhood. Her resentment against David,
for some reason unknown to Letty, was deep and
profound and she made no secret of it; until the
outraged Letty, goaded into speech one day, said:
"Listen, Eva! David brought you here because his
sister's house was the proper place for you just
now. I don't know why you married each other,
but you did, and it's evidently a failure. I'm
going to stand by David and see you through
this trouble, but while you're under my roof

you'll have to speak respectfully of my brother;
not so much because he's my brother, but because he's your husband and the father of the
child that's coming:—do you understand?"

Letty had a good deal of red in her bronze hair
and her brown eyes were as capable of flashing
fire as Eva's black ones; so the girl not only re-
frained from venting her spleen upon the absent
David, but ceased to talk altogether, and the
gloom in the house was as black as if Mrs. Popham and all her despondent ancestors were living
under its roof.

The good doctor called often and did his best,
shrugging his shoulders and lifting his eyebrows
as he said: "Let her work out her own salvation. I
doubt if she can, but we'll give her the chance. If
the problem can be solved, the child will do it."

IV

WELL, the problem never was solved, never in this world, at least; and those who were in the sitting-room chamber when Eva was shown her two babies lying side by side on a pillow, never forgot the quick glance of horrified incredulity, or the shriek of aversion with which she greeted them.

Letty had a sense of humor, and it must be confessed that when the scorned and discarded babies were returned to her, and she sat by the kitchen stove trying to plan a second bottle, a second cradle, and see how far the expected baby could divided it modest outfit with the unexpected one, she burst into a fit of hysterical laughter mingled with an outpour of tears.

The doctor came in from the sick-room puz-

++++++++++++++++++++++++++++++++++++

zled and crestfallen from his interview with an entirely new specimen of womankind. He had brought Letty and David into the world and soothed the last days of all her family, and now in this tragedy—for tragedy it was—he was her only confidant and adviser.

Letty looked at him, the tears streaming from her eyes.

"Oh, Doctor Lee, Doctor Lee! If an overruling Providence could smile, would n't He smile now? David and Eva never wanted to marry each other, I'm sure of it, and the last thing they desired was a child. Now there are two of them. Their father is away, their mother won't look at them! What will become of me until Eva gets well and behaves like a human being? I never promised to be an aunt to twins; I never did like twins; I think they're downright vulgar!"

"Waly waly! bairns are bonny:
One's enough and twa's ower mony,"

quoted the doctor. "It's worse even than you think, my poor Letty, for the girl can't get well, because she won't! She has gritted her teeth, turned her face to the wall, and refused her food.

++

It's the beginning of the end. You are far likelier to be a foster mother than an aunt!"

Letty's face changed and softened and her color rose. She leaned over the two pink, crumpled creatures, still twitching nervously with the amazement and discomfort of being alive.

"Come to your Aunt Letty then and be mothered!" she sobbed, lifting the pillow and taking it, with its double burden, into her arms. "You shan't suffer, poor innocent darlings, even if those who brought you into the world turn away from you! Come to your Aunt Letty and be mothered!"

"That's right, that's right," said the doctor over a lump in his throat. "We must n't let the babies pay the penalty of their parents' sins; and there's one thing that may soften your anger a little, Letty: Eva's not right; she's not quite responsible. There are cases where motherhood, that should be a joy, brings nothing but mental torture and perversion of instinct. Try and remember that, if it helps you any. I'll drop in every two or three hours and I'll write David to come at once. He must take his share of the burden."

Well, David came, but Eva was in her coffin.

++

He was grave and silent, and it could not be said that he showed a trace of fatherly pride. He was very young, it is true, thoroughly ashamed of himself, very unhappy, and anxious about his new cares; but Letty could not help thinking that he regarded the twins as a sort of personal insult,—perhaps not on their own part, nor on Eva's, but as an accident that might have been prevented by a competent Providence. At any rate, he carried himself as a man with a grievance, and when he looked at his offspring, which was seldom, it seemed to Letty that he regarded the second one as an unnecessary intruder and cherished a secret resentment at its audacity in coming to this planet uninvited. He went back to his work in Boston without its having crossed his mind that anybody but his sister could take care of his children. He did n't really regard them as children or human beings; it takes a woman's vision to make that sort of leap into the future. Until a newborn baby can show some personal beauty, evince some intellect, stop squirming and squealing, and exhibit enough self-control to let people sleep at night, it is not, as a rule, *persona grata* to any one but its mother.

David did say vaguely to Letty when he was leaving, that he hoped "they would be good," the screams that rent the air at the precise moment of farewell rather giving the lie to his hopes.

Letty was struggling to end the interview without breaking down, for she was worn out nervously as well as physically, and thought if she could only be alone with her problems and her cares she would rather write to David than tell him her mind face to face.

Brother and sister held each other tightly for a moment, kissed each other good-bye, and then Letty watched Osh Popham's sleigh slipping off with David into the snowy distance, the merry tinkle of the bells adding to the sadness in her dreary heart. Dick gone yesterday, Dave to-day; Beulah without Dick and Dave! The two joys of her life were missing and in their places two unknown babies whose digestive systems were going to need constant watching, according to Dr. Lee. Then she went about with set lips, doing the last sordid things that death brings in its wake; doing them as she had seen her mother do before her. She threw away the husks in Eva's under mattress and put fresh ones in; she emptied the feathers from the feather bed and pillows and aired them in the sun while she washed the ticking; she scrubbed the paint in the sickroom,

and in between her tasks learned from Clarissa
Perry the whole process of bringing up babies by
hand.

That was three years ago. At first David had
sent ten dollars a month from his slender earn-
ings, never omitting it save for urgent reasons.
He evidently thought of the twins as "company"
for his sister and their care a pleasant occupation,
since she had "almost" a living income; taking in
a few coats to make, just to add an occasional
luxury to the bare necessities of life provided by
her mother's will.

His letters were brief, dispirited, and infre-
quent, but they had not ceased altogether till
within the last few months, during which Letty's
to him had been returned from Boston with
"Not found" scribbled on the envelopes.

The firm in whose care Letty had latterly ad-
dressed him simply wrote, in answer to her in-
quiries, that Mr. Gilman had not been in their
employ for some time and they had no idea of his
whereabouts.

The rest was silence.

V

A GOOD deal of water had run under Beulah Bridge since Letty Boynton had sat at her window on a December evening unconsciously furnishing copy and illustration for a Christmas card; yet there had been very few outward changes in the village. Winter had melted into spring, burst into summer, faded into autumn, lapsed into winter again,— the same old, ever-recurring pageant in the world of Nature, and the same procession of incidents in the neighborhood life.

The harvest moon and the hunter's moon had come and gone; the first frost, the family dinners and reunions at Thanksgiving, the first snowfall; and now, as Christmas approached, the same holiday spirit was abroad in the air, slightly modi-

fied as it passed by Mrs. Popham's mournful
visage.

One or two babies had swelled the census,
giving the minister hope of a larger Sunday-
School; one or two of the very aged neighbors
had passed into the beyond; and a few romantic
and enterprising young farmers had espoused
wives, among them Osh Popham's son.

The manner of their choice was not entirely to
the liking of the village. Digby Popham had
married into the rival church and as his be-
trothed was a masterful young lady it was feared
that Digby would leave Mr. Larrabee's flock to
worship with his wife. Another had married
without visible means of support, a proceeding
always to be regretted by thoroughly prudent
persons over fifty; and the third, Deacon Todd's
eldest son, had somehow or other met a siren
from Vermont and insisted on wedding her when
there were plenty of marriageable girls in Beulah.

"I've no patience with such actions!" grum-
bled Mrs. Popham. "Young folks are so full of
notions nowadays that they look for change and
excitement everywheres. I s'pose James Todd
thinks it's a decent, respectable way of actin', to
turn his back on the girls he's been brought up

an' gone to school with, and court somebody he
never laid eyes on till a year ago. It's a free country, but I must say I don't think it's very refined
for a man to go clear off somewheres and marry a
perfect stranger!"

Births, marriages, and deaths, however, paled
into insignificance compared with the spectacu-
lar début of the minister's wife as a writer and
embellisher of Christmas cards, two at least having been seen at the local milliner's store. How
many she had composed, and how many of them
(said Mrs. Popham) might have been rejected,
nobody knew, though there was much specula-
tion; and more than one citizen remarked on the
size of the daily package of mail matter handed
out by the rural delivery man at the parsonage
gate.

No one but Mrs. Larrabee and Letty Boynton
were in possession of all the thrilling details at-
tending the public appearance of these works of
art; the words and letters of appreciation, the
commendation, and the occasional blows to
pride that attended their acceptance and publica-
tion.

Mrs. Larrabee's first attempt, with the sketch
of Letty at the window on Christmas Eve, her
hearth-fire aglow, her heart and her door open

that Love might enter in if the Christ Child
came down the snowy street,—this went to the
Excelsior Card Company in a large Western city,
and the following correspondence ensued:

MRS. LUTHER LARRABEE,
    Beulah, N.H.

DEAR MADAM:—

Your letter bears a well-known postmark,
for my father and my grandfather were born
and lived in New Hampshire, "up Beulah
way." I accept your verses because of the
beauty of the picture that accompanied them,
and because Christmas means more than holly
and plum pudding and gift-laden trees to me,
for I am a religious man,—a ministerial father
and three family deacons saw to that, though
it does n't always work that way!—Frankly, I
do not expect your card to have a wide appeal,
so I offer you only five dollars.

A Christmas card, my dear madam, must
have a greeting, and yours has none. If the
pictured room were a real room, and some one
who had seen or lived in it should recognize
it, it would attract his eye, but we cannot

manufacture cards to meet such romantic im-
probabilities. I am emboldened to ask you
(because you live in Beulah) if you will not
paint the outside of some lonely, little New
Hampshire cottage, as humble as you like,
and make me some more verses; something,
say, about "the folks back home."

Sincerely yours,

REUBEN SMALL.

BEULAH, N.H.

DEAR MR. SMALL:—

I accept your offer of five dollars for my
maiden effort in Christmas cards with thanks,
and will try my hand at something more popular. I am not above liking to make a "wide
appeal," but the subject you propose is rather
a staggering one, because you accompany it
with a phrase lacking rhythm, and difficult to
rhyme. You will at once see, by running
through the alphabet, that "roam" is the only
serviceable rhyme for "*home*," but the union
of the two suggests jingle or doggerel. I defy
any minor poet when furnished with such
a phrase, to refrain from bursting at once into:—

++++++++++++++++++++++++++++++++++++++

No matter where you travel, no matter
where you roam,
You'll never dum-di-dum-di-dee
    The folks back home.

            Sincerely yours,
                    REBA LARRABEE.

P.S. On second thought I believe James
Whitcomb Riley could do it and overcome the
difficulties, but alas! I have not his touch!

DEAR MRS. LARRABEE:—

We never refuse verses because they are too
good for the public. Nothing is too good for
the public, but the public must be the judge
of what pleases it.

"The folks back home" is a phrase that will
strike the eye and ear of thousands of wander-
ing sons and daughters. They will choose that
card from the heaped-up masses on the
counters and send it to every State in the
Union. If you will glance at your first card
you will see that though people may read it
they will always leave it on the counter. I
want my cards on counters, by the thousand,

++++++++++++++++++++++++++++++++++++++

++

but I don't intend that they should be left there!

Make an effort, dear Mrs. Larrabee! I could get "the folks back home" done here in the office in half an hour, but I'm giving you the chance because you live in Beulah, New Hampshire, and because you make beautiful pictures.

Sincerely yours,

REUBEN SMALL.

DEAR MR. SMALL:—

I enclose a colored sketch of the outside of the cottage whose living-room I used in my first card. I chose it because I love the person who lives in it; because it always looks beautiful in the snow, and because the tree is so picturesque. The fact that it is gray for lack of paint may remind a casual wanderer that there is something to do, now and then, for the "folks back home." The verse is just as bad as I thought it would be. It seems incredible that any one should buy it, but ours is a big country and there are many kinds of people living in it, so who knows? Why don't you accept my picture and then you write the

++

card? I could not put my initials on this! They
are unknown, to be sure, and I should want
them to be, if you use it!

Sincerely yours,

REBA LARRABEE.

Now here's a Christmas greeting
　　To the "folks back home."
It comes to you across the space,
　　Dear folks back home!
I've searched the wide world over,
　　But no matter where I roam,
No friends are like the old friends,
　　No folks like those back home!

DEAR MRS. LARRABEE:—

I gave you five dollars for the first picture
and verses, which you, as a writer, regard
more highly than I, who am merely a manu-
facturer. Please accept twenty dollars for "The
Folks Back Home," on which I hope to make
up my loss on the first card! I insist on sign-
ing the despised verse with your initials. In
case R.L. should later come to mean some-

thing, you will be glad that a few thousand
people have seen it.

Sincerely,

REUBEN SMALL.

The Hessian soldier andirons, the portrait over
the Boynton mantel, and even Letty Boynton's
cape were identified on the first card, sooner or
later, but it was obvious that Mrs. Larrabee had
to have a picture for her verses and could n't be
supposed to make one up "out of her head";
though Osh Popham declared it had been done
again and again in other parts of the world. Also
it was agreed that, as Letty's face was not distin-
guishable, nobody outside of Beulah could recognize her by her cape; and that anyhow it could
n't make much difference, for if anybody wanted
to spend fifteen cents on a card he would certainly buy the one about "the folks back home."
The popularity of this was established by the fact
that it was selling, not only in Beulah and
Greentown, but in Boston, and in Racine, Wisconsin, and, it was rumored, even in Chicago.
The village milliner in Beulah had disposed of
twenty-seven copies in thirteen days and the
minister's wife was universally conceded to be

the most celebrated person in the State of New Hampshire.

Letty Boynton had an uncomfortable moment when she saw the first card, but common sense assured her that outside of a handful of neighbors no one would identify her home surroundings; meantime she was proud of Reba's financial and artistic triumph in "The Folks Back Home" and generously glad that she had no share in it.

Twice during the autumn David had broken his silence, but only to send her a postal from some Western town, telling her that he should have no regular address for a time; that he was traveling for a publishing firm and felt ill-adapted to the business. He hoped that she and the children were well, for he himself was not; etc., etc.

The twins had been photographed by Osh Popham, who was Jack of all trades and master of many, and a sight of their dimpled charms, curly heads, and straight little bodies would have gladdened any father's heart, Letty thought. However, she scorned to win David back by any such specious means. If he did n't care to know whether his children were hump-backed, bow-legged, cross-eyed, club-footed, or feeble-minded, why should she enlighten him? This was her usual frame of mind, but in these last days of the year how she longed to pop the bewitching photographs and Reba's Christmas cards into an envelope and send them to David.

But where? No word at all for weeks and weeks, and then only a postal from St. Joseph, saying that he had given up his position on account of poor health. Nothing in all this to keep Christmas on, thought Letty, and she knitted and crocheted and sewed with extra ardor that the twins' stockings might be filled with bright things of her own making.

VI

ON the afternoon before Christmas of that year, the North Station in Boston was filled with hurrying throngs on the way home for the holidays. Everybody looked tired and excited, but most of them had happy faces, and men and women alike had as many bundles as they could carry; bundles and boxes quite unlike the brown paper ones with which commuters are laden on ordinary days. These were white packages, beribboned and beflowered and behollied and bemistletoed, to be gently carried and protected from crushing.

The train was filled to overflowing and many stood in the aisles until Latham Junction was reached and the overflow alighted to change cars for Greentown and way stations.

Among the crowd were two men with suit-

cases who hurried into the way train and, entering the smoking car from opposite ends, met in
the middle of the aisle, dropped their encum-
brances, stretched out a hand and exclaimed in
the same breath:

"Dick Larrabee, upon my word!"

"Dave Gilman, by all that's great!—Here,
let's turn over a seat for our baggage and sit together. Going home, I s'pose?"

The men had not met for some years, but each
knew something of the other's circumstances and
hoped that the other did n't know too much.
They scanned each other's faces, Dick thinking
that David looked pinched and pale, David half-
heartedly registering the quick impression that
Dick was prosperous.

"Yes," David answered; "I'm going home for a
couple of days. It's such a confounded journey to
that one-horse village that a business man can't
get there but once in a generation!"

"Awful hole!" confirmed Dick. "Simply awful
hole! I did n't get it out of my system for years."

"Married?" asked David.

"No; rather think I'm not the marrying kind,
though the fact is I've had no time for love affairs—too busy. Let's see, you have a child, have
n't you?"

"Yes; Letty has seen to all that business for me since my wife died." (Wild horses could n't have dragged the information from him that the "child" was "twins," and Dick did n't need it anyway, for he had heard the news the morning he left Beulah.) "Wonder if there have been many changes in the village?"

"Don't know; there never used to be! Mrs. Popham has been ailing for years,—she could n't die; and Deacon Todd would n't!" Dick's old animosities still lingered faintly in his memory, though his laughing voice and the twinkle in his eyes showed plainly that no bitterness was left. "How's business with you, David?"

"Only so-so. I've had the devil's own luck lately. Can't get anything that suits me or that pays a decent income. I formed a new connection the other day, but I can't say yet what there is in it. I'm just out of hospital; operation; they cut out the wrong thing first, I believe, sewed me up absent-mindedly, then remembered it was the other thing, and did it over again. At any rate, that's the only way I can account for their mewing me up there for two months."

"Well, well, that is hard luck! I'm sorry, old boy! Things did n't begin to go my way either till within the last few months. I've always made a fair living and saved a little money, but never gained any real headway. Now I've got a first-rate start and the future looks pretty favorable, and best of all, pretty safe.— No trouble at home calls you back to Beulah? I hope Letty is all right?" Dick cast an anxious side glance at David, though he spoke carelessly.

"Oh, no! Everything's serene, so far as I know. I'm a poor correspondent, especially when I've no good news to tell; and anyway, the mere sight of a pen ties my tongue. I'm just running down to surprise Letty."

Dick looked at David again. He began to think he did n't like him. He used to, when they were boys, but when he brought that unaccountable wife home and foisted her and her babies on Letty, he rather turned against him. David was younger than himself, four or five years younger, but he looked as if he had n't grown up. Surely his boyhood chum had n't used to be so pale and thin-chested or his mouth so ladylike and pretty. A good face, though; straight and clean, with honest eyes and a likeable smile. Lack of will, perhaps, or a persistent run of ill luck. Letty had always kept him stiffened up in the old days. Dick recalled one of his father's phrases to the

effect that Dave Gilman would spin on a very
small biscuit, and wondered if it were still true.

"And you, Dick? Your father's still living?
You see I have n't kept up with Beulah lately."

"Keeping up with Beulah! It sounds like the
title of a novel, but the hero would have to be a
snail or he'd pass Beulah in the first chapter!—
Yes, father's hale and hearty, I believe."

"You come home every Christmas, I s'pose?"
inquired David.

"No; as a matter of fact this is my first visit
since I left for good."

"That's about my case." And David hung his
head a little, unconsciously.

"That so? Well, I was a hot-headed fool when
I said good-bye to Beulah, and it's taken me all
this time to cool off and make up my mind to
apologize to the dad. There's—there's rather a
queer coincidence about my visit just at this
time."

"Speaking of coincidences," said David, "I can
beat yours, whatever it is. If the thought of your
father brought you back, my mother drew me—
this way!" And he took something from his inside coat pocket.—"Do you see that?"

Dick regarded the object blankly, then with a

quick gesture dived into his pocket and brought forth another of the same general character. "How about this?" he asked.

Each had one of Reba Larrabee's Christmas cards but David had the first unsuccessful one and Dick the popular one with the lonely little gray house and the verse about the folks back home.

The men looked at each other in astonishment and Dick gave a low whistle. Then they bent over the cards together.

"It was mother's picture that pulled me back to Beulah, I don't mind telling you," said David, his mouth twitching. "Don't you see it?"

"Oh! Is that your mother?" And Dick scanned the card closely.

"Don't you remember her portrait that always hung there after she died?"

"Yes, of course!" And Dick's tone was apologetic. "You see the face is so small I did n't notice it, but I recognize it now and remember the portrait."

"Then the old sitting-room!" exclaimed David. "Look at the rag carpet and the blessed old andirons! Gracious! I've crawled round those Hessian soldiers, burned my fingers and cracked my skull on 'em, often enough when I was a kid!

When I'd studied the card five minutes, I bought a ticket and started for home."

David's eyes were suffused and his lip trembled.

"I don't wonder," said Dick. "I recognize the dear old room right enough, and of course I should know Letty."

"It did n't occur to me that it *was* Letty for some time," said her brother. "There's just the glimpse of a face shown, and no real likeness."

"Perhaps not," agreed Dick. "A stranger would n't have known it for Letty, but if it had been only that cape I should have guessed. It's as familiar as Mrs. Popham's bugle bonnet, and much prettier. She wore it every winter,—skating, you know,—and it's just the color of her hair."

"Letty has a good-shaped head," said David judicially. "It shows, even in the card."

"And a remarkable ear," added Dick, "so small and so close to her head."

"I never notice people's ears," confessed David.

"Don't you? I do, and eyelashes, too. Mother's got Letty's eyelashes down fine.—She's changed, Dave, Letty has! That hurts me. She was always so gay and chirpy. In this picture she has a sad, faraway, listening look, but mother may have put that in just to make it interesting."

"Or perhaps I've had something to do with the change of expression!" thought David. "What attracted me first," he added, "was your mother's verses. She always had a knack of being pious without cramming piety down your throat. I liked that open door. It meant welcome, no matter how little you'd deserved it."

"Where'd you get your card, Dave?" asked Dick. "It's prettier than mine."

"A nurse brought it to me in the hospital just because she took a fancy to it. She did n't know it would mean anything to me, but it did—a relapse!" And David laughed shamedfacedly. "I guess she'll confine herself to beef tea after this! —Where'd you get yours?"

"Picked it up on a dentist's mantelpiece when I was waiting for an appointment. I was traveling round the room, hands in my pockets, when suddenly I saw this card standing up against an hour-glass. The color caught me. I took it to the window, and at first I was puzzled. It certainly was Letty's house. The door's open, you see, and there's somebody in the window. I knew it was Letty, but how could any card publisher have found the way to Beulah? Then I discovered mother's initials snarled up in holly, and remembered that she was always painting and illuminating."

"Queer job, life is!" said David, putting his card back in his pocket and wishing there were a little more time, or that he had a little more courage, so that he might confide in Dick Larrabee. He felt a desire to tell him some of the wretchedness he had lived through. It would be a comfort just to hint that his unhappiness had made him a coward, so that the very responsibilities that serve as a spur to some men had left him until now cold, unstirred, unvitalized.

"You're right!" Dick answered. "Life is a queer job and it does n't do to shirk it. And just as queer as anything in life is the way that mother's Christmas cards brought us back to Beulah! They acted as a sort of magic, did n't they?—Jiminy! I believe the next station is Beulah. I hope the depot team will be hitched up."

"Yes, here we are; seven o'clock and the train only thirty-five minutes late. It always made a point of that on holidays!"

"Never mind!" And Dick's tone was as gay as David's was sober. "The beanpot will have gone back to the cellarway and the doughnuts to the crock, but the 'folks back home' 'll get 'em out for us, and a mince pie, too, and a cut of sage cheese."

"There won't be any 'folks back home,' we're so late, I'm thinking. There's always a Christmas Eve festival at the church, you know. They never change—in Beulah."

"Then, by George, they can have me for Santa Claus!" said Dick as they stepped out on the platform. "Why, it does n't seem cold at all; yet look at the ice on the river! What skating, and what a moon! My blood's up, and if I find the parsonage closed, I'll follow on to the church and make my peace with the members. There's a kind of spell on me! For the first time in years I feel as though I could shake hands with Deacon Todd."

"Well, Merry Christmas to you, Dick,—I'm going to walk. Good gracious! Have you come to spend the winter?" For various bags and parcels were being flung out on the platform with that indifference and irresponsibility that bespeak the touch of the seasoned baggage-handler.

"You did n't suppose I was coming back to Beulah empty-handed, on Christmas Eve, did you? If I'm in time for the tree, I'm going to give those blue-nosed, frost-bitten little youngsters something to remember! Jump in, Dave, and ride as far as the turn of the road."

In a few minutes the tottering old signboard that marked the way to Beulah Center hove in sight, and David jumped from the sleigh to take his homeward path.

"Merry Christmas again, Dick!" he waved.

"Same to you, Dave! I'll come myself to say it to Letty the first minute I see smoke coming from your chimney tomorrow morning. Tell her you met me, will you, and that my visit is partly for her, only that father had to have his turn first. She'll know why. Tell her mother's card had Christmas magic in it, tell—"

"Say, tell her the rest yourself, will you, Dick?" And Dave broke into a run down the hill road that led to Letty.

"I will, indeed!" breathed Dick into his muffler.

VII

REPEATING history, Letty was again at her open window. She had been half-ashamed to reproduce the card, as it were, but something impelled her. She was safe from scrutiny, too, for everybody had gone to the tree—the Pophams, Mr. Davis, Clarissa Perry, everybody for a quarter of a mile up and down the street, and by now the company would be gathered and the tree lighted. She could keep watch alone, the only sound being that of the children's soft breathing in the next room.

Letty had longed to go to the festival herself, but old Clarissa Perry, who cared for the twins now and then in Letty's few absences, had a niece who was going to "speak a piece," and she yearned to be present and share in the glory; so Letty was kept at home as she had been numberless other times during the three years of her vicarious motherhood.

The night was mild again, as in the year before. The snow lay like white powder on the hard earth; the moon was full, and the street was a length of dazzling silence. The lighted candle was in the parlor window, shining toward the meeting-house, the fire burned brightly on the hearth, the front door was ajar. Letty wrapped her old cape round her shoulders, drew her hood over her head, and seating herself at the window repeated under her breath:—

> "My door is on the latch to-night,
>   The hearth-fire is aglow.
> I seem to hear swift passing feet,
>   The Christ Child in the snow.
>
> "My heart is open wide to-night
>   For stranger, kith, or kin;
> I would not bar a single door
>   Where Love might enter in!"

And then a footstep, drawing ever nearer, sounded crunch, crunch, in the snow. Letty pushed the chair back into the shadow. The footstep halted at the gate, came falteringly up the path, turned aside, and came nearer the window. Then a voice said: "Don't be frightened Letty, it's David! Can I come in? I have n't any right to, except that it's Christmas Eve."

That, indeed, was the magic, the all-comprehending phrase that swept the past out of mind with one swift stroke: the acknowledgment of unworthiness, the childlike claim on the forgiving love that should be in every heart on such a night as this. Resentment melted away like mist before the sun. Her deep grievance—where had it gone? How could she speak anything but welcome? For what was the window open, the fire lighted, the door ajar, the guiding candle-flame, but that Love, and David, might enter in?

There were few words at first; nothing but close-locked hands and wet cheeks pressed together. Then Letty sent David into the children's room by himself. If the twins were bewitching when awake, they were nothing short of angelic when asleep.

David came out a little later, his eyes reddened with tears, his hair rumpled, his face flushed. He seemed like a man awed by an entirely new experience. He could not speak, he could only stammer brokenly:—

"As God is my witness, Letty, there's been something wrong with me up to this moment. I never thought of them as my children before, and I can't believe that such as they can belong to me. They were never wanted, and I've never had any interest in them. I owe them to you, Letty; you've made them what they are; you, and no one else."

"If there had n't been something there to build on, my love and care would n't have counted for much. They're just like dear mother's people for good looks and brains and pretty manners: they're pure Shirley all the way through, the twinnies are."

"It's lucky for me that they are!" said David humbly. "You see, Letty, I married Eva to keep my promise. If I was old enough to make it, I was old enough to keep it, so I thought. She never loved me, and when she found out that I did n't love her any longer she turned against me. Our life together was awful, from beginning to end, but she's in her grave, and nobody'll ever hear my side, now that she can't tell hers. When I looked at those two babies the day I left you, I thought of them only as retribution; and the vision of them—ugly, wrinkled, writhing little creatures—has been in my mind ever since."

"They were compensation, not retribution, David. I ought to have told you how clever and beautiful they were, but you never asked and my pride was up in arms. A man should stand by his own flesh and blood, even if it is n't attractive; that's what I believe."

"I know, I know! But I've had no feeling for three years. I've been like a frozen man, just drifting, trying to make both ends meet, my heart dead and my body full of pain. I'm just out of a hospital — two months in all."

"David! Why did n't you let me know, or send for me?"

"Oh, it was way out in Missouri. I was taken ill very suddenly at the hotel in St. Joseph and they moved me at once. There were two operations first and last, and I did n't know enough to feed myself most of the time."

"Poor, poor Buddy! Did you have good care?"

"The best. I had more than care. Ruth Bentley, the nurse that brought me back to life, made me see what a useless creature I was."

Some woman's instinct stirred in Letty at a new note in her brother's voice and a new look in his face. She braced herself for his next words, sure that they would open a fresh chapter. The door and the window were closed now, the

++

shades pulled down, the fire low; the hour was ripe for confidences.

"You see, Letty,"—and David cleared his throat nervously, and looked at the coals gleaming behind the Hessian soldiers,—"it's a time for a thorough housecleaning, body, mind, and soul, a long illness is; and Miss Bentley knew well enough that all was wrong with me. I mentioned my unhappy marriage and told her all about you, but I said nothing about the children."

"Why should you?" asked Letty, although her mind had leaped to the reason already.

"Well, I was a poor patient in one of the cheapest rooms; broken in health, without any present means of support. I wanted to stand well with her, she had been so good to me, and I thought if she knew about the twins she would n't believe I could ever make a living for three."

"Still less for *four!*" put in Letty, with an irrepressible note of teasing in her tone.

She had broken the ice. Like a torrent set free, David dashed into the story of the last two months and Ruth Bentley's wonderful influence. How she had recreated him within as well as without. How she was the best and noblest of women, willing to take a pauper by the hand and brace him up for a new battle with life.

++

"Strength appeals to me," confessed David. "Perhaps it's because I am weak; for I'm afraid I am, a little!"

"Be careful, Davy! Eva was strong!"

David shuddered. He remembered a strength that lashed and buffeted and struck and overpowered.

"Ruth is different," he said. "'Out of the strong came forth sweetness' used to be one of Parson Larrabee's texts. That's Ruth's kind of strength.—Can I—will you let me bring her here to see you, Letty,—say for New Year's? It's all so different from the last time I asked you. Then I knew I was bringing you nothing but sorrow and pain, but Ruth carries her welcome in her face."

The prop inside of Letty wavered unsteadily for a moment and then stood in its accustomed upright position.

"Why not?" she asked. "It's the right thing to do; but you must tell her about the children first."

"Oh! I did that long ago, after I found out that she cared. It was only at first that I did n't dare. I have n't told you, but she went out for her daily walk and brought me home a Christmas card, the prettiest one she could find,

she said. I was propped up on pillows, as weak as
a kitten. I looked at it and looked at it, and
when I saw that it was this room, the old fireplace and mother's picture, and the Hessian soldier andirons, when I realized there was a face at
the window and that the door was ajar,—everything just swam before me and I fainted dead
away. I had a relapse, and when I was better
again I told her everything. She's fond of children. It did n't make any difference, except for
her to say that the more she had to do for me,
the more she wanted to do it."

"Well," said Letty with a break in her voice,
"that's love, so far as I can see, and if you've been
lucky enough to win it, take it and be thankful,
and above all, nurse and keep it.— So one of
Reba's cards, the one the publisher thought
would never sell, found you and brought you
back! How wonderful! We little thought of that,
Reba and I!"

"Reba's work did n't stop there, Letty! There
was so much that had to be said between you and
me, just now, that I could n't let another subject
creep in till it was finished and we were friends;
—but Dick Larrabee saw Reba's card about 'the
folks back home' in Chicago and he bought a

ticket for Beulah just as I did. We met in the train and compared notes."

"Dick Larrabee home?"

The blood started in Letty's heart and sped hither and thither, warming her from head to foot.

"Yes, looking as fit as a fiddle; the way a man looks when things are coming his way."

"But what did the card mean to him? Did he seem to like Reba's verses?"

"Yes, but I guess the card just spelled home to him; and he recognized this house in a minute, of course. I showed him my card and he said: 'That's Letty fast enough: I know the cape.' He recognized you in a minute, he said."

He knew the cape! Yes, the old cape had been close to his shoulder many a time. He liked it and said it matched her hair.

"He was awfully funny about your ear, too! I told him I never noticed women's ears, and he said he did, when they were pretty, and their eyelashes, too.— Anything remarkable about your eyelashes, Letty?"

"Nothing that I'm aware of!" said Letty laughingly, although she was fibbing and she knew it.

"And he said he'd call and say 'Merry Christmas' to you the first thing tomorrow; that he would have been here to-night but you'd know his father had to come first. You don't mind being second to the parson, do you?"

No, Letty did n't mind. Her heart was unaccountably light and glad, like a girl's heart. It was the Eve of Mary when all women are blest because of one. The Wise Men brought gifts to the Child; Letty had often brought hers timidly, devoutly, trustfully, and perhaps to-night they were coming back to her!

VIII

PUT the things down on the front steps," said Dick to the driver as he neared the parsonage. "If there's nobody at home I'll go on up to the church after I've got this stuff inside."

"Got a key?"

"No, don't need one. I've picked all the locks with a penknife many a time. Besides, the key is sure to be under the doormat. Yes, here it is! Of all the unaccountable customs I ever knew, that's the most laughable!"

"Works all right for you!"

"Yes, and for all the other tramps,"—and Dick opened the door and lifted in his belongings. "Good-night," he called to the driver; "I'll walk up to the church after I've found out

+++++++++++++++++++++++++++++++++++
75

whether mother keeps the mince pie and cider apple sauce in the same old place."

A few minutes later, his hunger partially stayed, Dick Larrabee locked the parsonage door and took the well-trodden path across the church common. It was his father's feet, he knew, that had worn the shoveled path so smooth; his kind, faithful feet that had sped to and fro on errands of mercy, never faltering in all the years.

It was nearly eight o'clock. The sound of the melodeon, with children's voices, floated out from the white-painted meeting-house, all ablaze with light; or as much ablaze as a kerosene chandelier and six side lamps could make it. The horse sheds were crowded with teams of various sorts, the horses well blanketed and standing comfortably in straw; and the last straggler was entering the right-hand door of the church as Dick neared the steps. Simultaneously the left-hand door opened, and on the background of the light inside appeared the figure of Mrs. Todd, the wife of his ancient enemy, the senior deacon. Dick could see that sort of dressing-room had been curtained off in the little entry, as it had often been in former times of tableaux and concerts and what not. Valor, not discretion, was the better policy, and walking boldly up to the steps Dick took off his fur cap and said, "Good-evening, Mrs. Todd!"

"Good gracious me! Where under the canopy did you hail from, Dick Larrabee? Was your folks lookin' for you? They ain't breathed a word to none of us."

"No, I'm a surprise, Mrs. Todd."

"Well, I know you've given me one! Will you wait a spell till the recitations is over? You'd scare the children so, if you go in now, that they'd forget their pieces more'n they gen'ally do."

"I can endure the loss of the 'pieces,'" said Dick with a twinkle in his eye.

At which Mrs. Todd laughed comprehendingly, and said: "Isaac'll get a stool or a box or something; there ain't a vacant seat in the church. I wish we could say the same o' Sundays!—Issac! Issac! Come out and see who's here," she called under her breath. "He won't be long. He's tendin' John Trimble in the dressin'-room. He was the only one in the village that was willin' to be Santa Claus an' he wa'n't over-willin'. Now he's et something for supper that disagrees with him awfully and he's all doubled up with colic. We can't have the tree till the exercises is over, but that won't be mor'n fifteen minutes, so I sent Issac home to make a mustard plaster. He's puttin' it on John now. John's dreadful solemn and unamusin' when he's well, and I can't think how he'll act when he's all crumpled up with stomach-ache, an' the mustard plaster drawin' like fire."

Dick threw back his head and laughed. He had forgotten just how unexpected Beulah's point of view always was.

Deacon Todd now came out cautiously.

"I've got it on him, mother, tho' he's terrible unresigned to it; an' I've given him a stiff dose o' Jamaica Ginger. We can tell pretty soon whether he can take his part."

"Here's Dick Larrabee come back, Issaac, just when we thought he had given up Beulah for good an' all!" said Mrs. Todd.

The Deacon stood on the top step, his gaunt, grizzled face peering above the collar of his great coat; not a man to eat his words very often, Deacon Issaac Todd.

"Well, young man," he said, "you've found your way home, have you? It's about time, if you want to see your father alive!"

"If it had n't been for you and others like you, men who had forgotten what it was to be young, I should never have gone away," said Dick hotly.

"What had I done worse than a dozen others, only that I happened to be the minister's son?"

"That's just it; you were bringin' trouble on the parish, makin' talk that reflected on your father. Folks said if he could n't control his own son, he wa'n't fit to manage a church. You played cards, you danced, you drove a fast horse."

"I never did a thing I'm ashamed of but one," —and Dick's voice was firm. "My misdeeds were nothing but boyish nonsense, but the village never gave me credit for a single virtue. I ought to have remembered father's position, but whatever I was or whatever I did, you had no right to pray for me openly for full five minutes at a public meeting. That galled me worse than anything!"

"Now, Isaac," interrupted Mrs. Todd. "I hope you'll believe me! I've told you once a week, on an average, these last three years, that you might have chastened Dick some other way besides prayin' for him in meetin'!"

The Deacon smiled grimly. "You both talk as if prayin' was one of the seven deadly sins," he said.

"I'm not objecting to your prayers," agreed Dick, "but there were plenty of closets in your house where you might have gone and told the Lord your opinion of me; only that was n't good enough for you; you must needs tell the whole village!"

"There, father, that's what I always said," agreed Mrs. Todd.

"Well, I ain't one that can't yield when the majority's against me," said the Deacon, "particularly when I'm treatin' John Trimble for the colic. If you'll stop actin' so you threaten to split the church, Dick Larrabee, I'll stop prayin' for you. The Lord knows how I feel about it now, so I need n't keep on remindin' Him."

IX

"WHAT'S a bargain and here's my hand on it," cried Dick. "Now, what do you say to lettin' me be Santa Claus? Come on in and let's look at John Trimble. He'd make a splendid Job or Jeremiah, but I would n't let him spoil a Christmas festival!"

"Do let Dick take the part, father,"—and Mrs. Todd's tone was most ingratiating. "John's terrible dull and bashful anyway, an' mebbe he'd have a pain he could n't stan' jest when he's givin' out the presents. An' Dick is always so amusin'."

Deacon Todd led the way into the improvised dressing-room. He had removed John's gala costume in order to apply the mustard faithfully and he lay in a crumpled heap in the corner. The plaster itself adorned a stool near by.

++

"Now, John! John! That plaster won't do you no good on the stool. It ain't the stool that needs drawin'; it's your stomach," argued Mrs. Todd.

"I'm drawed pretty nigh to death a'ready," moaned John. "I'm rore, that's what I am,— rore! An' I won't be Santa Claus neither. I want to go home."

"Wrop him up and get him into your sleigh, father, and take him home; then come right back. Bed's the place for him. Keep that hot flat-iron on his stomach, if he'd rather have it than the mustard. Men-folks are such cowards. I'll dress Dick while you're gone. Mebbe it's a Providence!"

On the whole, Dick agreed with Mrs. Todd as he stood ready to make his entrance. The School Committee was in the church and he had had much to do with its members in former days. The Selectmen of the village were present, and he had made their acquaintance once, in an executive session. The deacons were all there and the pillars of the church and the choir and the organist—a spinster who had actively disapproved when he had put beans in the melodeon one Sunday. Yes, it was best to meet them in a body on a festive occasion like this, when the rigors of the village point of view were relaxed. It would relieve him of several dozen private visits of apology, and altogether he felt that his courage would have wavered had he not been disguised as another person altogether: a popular favorite; a fat, jolly, rollicking dispenser of bounties to the general public. When he finally discarded his costume, would it not be easier, too, to meet his father first before the church full of people and have the solemn hour with him alone, later at night? Yes, as Mrs. Todd said, "Mebbe 't was a Providence!"

There was never such a merry Christmas festival in the Orthodox church of Beulah; everybody was of one mind as to that. There was a momentary fear that John Trimble, a pillar of prohibition, might have imbibed hard cider; so gay, so nimble, so mirth-provoking was Santa Claus. When was John Trimble ever known to unbend sufficiently to romp up the side aisle jingling his sleigh bells, and leap over a front pew stuffed with presents, to gain the vantage-ground he needed for the distribution of his pack? The wing pews on one side of the pulpit had been floored over and the Christmas Tree stood there, triumphant in beauty, while the gifts strewed the green-covered platform at its feet.

How gay, how audacious, how witty was
Santa Claus! How the village had always mis-
judged John Trimble, and how completely had
John Trimble hitherto obscured his light under a
bushel. In his own proper person children
avoided him, but they crowded about this Santa
Claus, encircling his legs, gurgling with joy
when they were lifted to his shoulder, their
laughter ringing through the church at his droll
antics. A sense of mystery grew when he opened
a pack on the pulpit stairs, a pack unfamiliar in
its outward aspect to the Committee on Enter-
tainment. Every girl had a little doll dressed in
fashionable attire, and every boy a brilliantly colored, splendidly noisy, tin trumpet; but hanging
to every toy by a red ribbon was Mrs. Larrabee's
Christmas card; her despised one about the "folks
back home."

The publisher's check to the minister's wife
had been accompanied by a dozen complimen-
tary copies, but these had been sent to Reba's
Western friends and relations; and although the
card was on many a marble-topped table in Beulah, it had not been bought by all the inhabi-
tants, by any means. Fifteen cents would
purchase something useful, and Beulah did not
contain may Crœsuses. Still, here the cards

were,—enough of them for everybody,—with a linen handkerchief for every woman and every man in the meeting-house, and a dozen more sticking out of the pack, as the people in the front pews could plainly see. Modest gifts, but plenty of them, and nobody knew from whence they came! There was a buzzing in the church, a buzzing that grew louder and more persistent when Santa Claus threw a lace scarf around Mrs. Larrabee's shoulders and approached her husband with a fine beaver collar in his hands: hands that trembled, as everybody could see, when he buttoned the piece of fur around the old minister's neck.

And the minister? He had been half in, and half out of, a puzzling dream for ten minutes, and when those hands of Santa Claus touched him, his flesh quivered. They reminded him of baby fingers that had crept around his neck years ago when he patiently walked the parsonage floor at night with his ailing child in his arms. Every drop of blood in his veins called out for answer. He looked above the white cotton beard and mustache to a pair of dark eyes; merry, mischievous, yet tender and soft; at a brown wavy lock escaping from the home-made wig. Then those who were near heard a weak voice say, "My

son!" and those who were far away observed
Santa Claus tear off his wig and beard, heard him
cry, "Father!"—and, as Mrs. Todd said afterwards, saw him "fall on to the minister's neck
right there before the whole caboodle, an' cling
to him for all the world like an engaged couple,
only they would n't 'a' made so free in public."

No ice but would have thawed in such an at-
mosphere! Grown-up Beulah forgot how much
trouble Dick Larrabee had caused in other days,
and the children had found a friend for all time.
The extraordinary number of dolls, trumpets,
handkerchiefs, and Christmas cards circulating
in the meeting-house raised the temperature con-
siderably, and induced a general feeling that if
Dick Larrabee had really ever been a bit wild and
reckless, he had evidently reformed, and pros-
pered, besides.

Yes, no one but a kind and omniscient Providence could have so beautifully arranged Dick
Larrabee's homecoming, and so wisely superin-
tended his complete reinstatement in the good
graces of Beulah village. A few maiden ladies felt
that he had been a trifle immodest in embracing,
and especially in kissing, his father in front of
the congregation; venturing the conviction that

kissing, an indecorous custom in any event, was especially lamentable in public.

"Pity Letty Boynton missed this evenin'," said Mrs. Todd. "Her an' Dick allers had a fancy for each other, so I've heard, though I don't know how true. Clarissa Perry might jest as well have stayed with the twins as not, for her niece that spoke a piece forgot 'bout half of it an' Clarissa was in a cold sweat every minute. Then the niece had a fit o' cryin', she was so ashamed at failin', an' Clarissa had to take her home. So they both missed the tree, an' Letty might 'a' been here as well as not an' got her handkerchief an' her card. I sent John Trimble's to him by the doctor, but he did n't take no notice, Isaac said, for the doctor was liftin' off the hot flat-iron an' puttin' turpentine on the spot where I'd had my mustard.—Anyway, if John had to have the colic he could n't 'a' chosen a better time, an' if he gets over it, I shall be real glad he had it; for nobody ever seen sech a Santa Claus as Dick Larrabee made, an' there never was, an' never will be, sech a lively, an' amusin' an' free-an'-easy evenin' in the Orthodox church."

X

"BLESS the card!" sighed David thankfully as he sat down to smoke a goodnight pipe and propped his feet contentedly against the little Hessian soldiers. The blaze of the logs on his own family hearthstone, after many months of steam heaters in the hall bedrooms of cheap hotels, how it soothed his tired heart and gave it visions of happiness to come! The card was on his knee, where he could look from its pictured scene to the real one of which he was again a glad and grateful part.

"Bless the card!" whispered Letty Boynton to herself as she went to her moonlit bedroom. Her eyes searched the snowy landscape and found the parsonage, "over the hills and far away." Then her heart flew like a bird across the distance and beat its wings in gladness, for a faint light streamed from the parson's study windows and she knew that father and son were together. That, in itself, was enough, with David sleeping under the home roof; but to-morrow was coming and to-morrow might be hers—her very own!

"Bless the card!" said Reba Larrabee, the tears shining in her eyes as she left the minister alone with his son. "Bless everybody and everything! Above all, bless God, 'from whom all blessings flow.'"

"Bless the card," said Dick Larrabee when he went up the narrow parsonage stairs to the room of his boyhood and found everything as it had been years ago. He leaned the little piece of paper magic against the mantel clock, threw it a kiss, and then, opening his pocket-book, he went nearer to the lamp and took out the faded tintype of a brown-haired girl in a brown cape. "Bless the card!" he said again, with a new note in his voice: "Bless the girl! And bless to-morrow if it brings me what I want most in all the world!"

About the Author

Best known for REBECCA OF SUNNYBROOK
FARM, Kate Douglas Wiggin (1865-1923) wrote
39 books, THE BIRDS' CHRISTMAS CAROL
among them. She argued for wholesomeness, not
hypocrisy, in fiction.